JUNE ARCHER is the President & CEO of Eleven28 Entertainment Group, a premier music and social media marketing consultant company in Hartford, Connecticut. Prior to establishing Eleven28 Entertainment, he was a member of the Elektra Records recording group Room Service. Archer is a staunch advocate in the fight to bring awareness to find a cure for AIDS and Breast Cancer and raises money through his annual June Archer's Celebration of Life event for these causes.

Go beyond the pages of
Yes! *Every Day Can Be A Good Day.*

Join the Yes! Community

JuneArcher.wordpress.com
JArcherInMyLifetime.Blogspot.com

www.Facebook.com/
YesEveryDayCanBeAGoodDay

Twitter / Instagram / Pinterest
@JuneArcher

UPTOWN BOOKS
Discover, Enrich & Inspire

ISBN: 978-1935883401

Written by June Archer
Foreward by Dr. Steve Perry and Anika Noni Rose
Creative Direction & Design by The Wright Design Group

Uptown Books November 2013
an imprint of **Augustus Publishing**

Uptown Books / Augustus Publishing 113 East 125th street NY, NY, 10035
AugustusPublishing.com | UptownMagazine.com

Foreward by **Dr. Steve Perry & Anika Noni Rose**

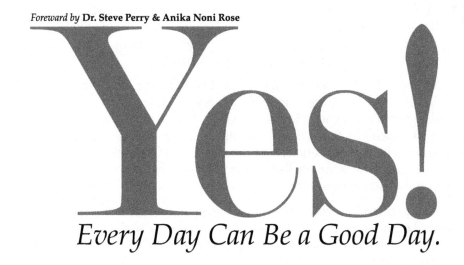

Yes!

Every Day Can Be a Good Day.

THE **KEYS TO SUCCESS**
THAT LEAD TO AN **AMAZING LIFE**

Foreward By
Dr. Steve Perry
(CNN Correspondent, TV Ones Host "Save My Son",
Principal at Capitol Prep Magnet School, Hartford, Ct)

The difference between success and failure is your perspective. Money will flow and dry up. Friends will come and go. And the spotlight, no matter how bright, will fade. Life is dynamic and that is why we need to be armed with a persistently positive perspective.

June Archer delivers a message that is only his to deliver. Each of us is blessed with something that distinguishes us. His gift is a palpable positivity. As you hold his words you should be feeling a rumbling of positivity that will set your sights on the best that life has to offer. He helps us construct the environment in which success need to occur with statements like, "True success is when you and those around you are successful."

I encourage you to take your time with these succulent morsels of wisdom. Let them melt in your mind as they feed your soul. Savor the joy of the search for your center, the perspective that will take you where you need to be.

I'm a school principal. My school is urban. My children are from the best and worst homes. They are the colors of America. Yet what sets them apart is not where they come from but where they are going. The best predictor of where they're going is not from where or who they come but how they look at life – perspective.

"Yes, Everyday Can Be A Good Day" offers people of all ages the most important determinant of success, a persistently positive perspective.

Foreward By
Anika Noni Rose
(Actress "Dreamgirls", "For Colored Girls", "Princess and The Frog")

For a long time, June was known at my house as 'The boy with the sparklee eyes' (you know parents & grandparents never remember names) and now that he's all grown up with children of his own, he's graduated to 'Sparklee Eyed June'. When he told me he was writing a book and wanted me to read it, I said sure; having no idea what it would be about. Now I know. June left home to pursue his dreams before I did, and it was years before we reconnected. But when we did, he looked just the same. He glows from the inside out.

This book is the secret behind those sparklee eyes. I always thought he was just happy-go-lucky (he is), but the truth is, he's joyous. Anyone who's spent time around him can attest to his joy, and the natural ability he has to spread it. But what I've learned here is that he also works at cultivating joy, and therefore success, within and all around him.

I hope you get to meet him some day, this man with the sparklee eyes. But if you don't do it in person, you can do it through these pages, and I bet you'll find (in ways big and/or small) that the answer is: YES! EVERYDAY CAN BE A GOOD DAY!

For

Magoo and Mama Bear

Acknowledgments

I'm no expert, but my aim is to MOTIVATE as many people who read this book as I can. I want you to realize your potential and be able to bring your dreams and aspirations to reality. The keys to success that I share come from experience, thoughts and a little common sense. I want those who read these keys to take at least the concepts and apply them in their daily lives as best they can. Creating success and maintaining it is all relative. Whether you're a janitor, an administrative assistant, manager or CEO, the same principles and ideas hold true. Some will find success faster than others. Some might find it easier than most people. There is one thing that remains constant, success requires work.

I hope this is the book that will help everyone make it thru the day. Just when you think every day can't be a good day, here are a few thoughts, observations and a touch of common sense to help change that perspective.

Special thanks to my mother, father, brother, grandmothers, grandfathers, grand aunts, aunts, uncles, cousins, mother and father in-law, brother and sister in-laws, nieces, nephews, godmothers, godfathers, god sisters, god brothers and all of my beautiful godchildren.

To Colin, Dely, Julian, Ronn P, Chris, Bema and Kevin thank you for making this journey a great experience at the times I needed to talk, take a road trip or telling me what I needed to hear and not what I wanted to hear. You are appreciated.

To All Purpose, my Augustus Publishing / Uptown Books team and Buzz Brand Marketing family. Thank you for listening to my ideas and helping make one of my dreams come true.

Ray Allen, Len Burnett, Wyclef Jean, Dr. Steve Perry, Anika Noni Rose, Attorney James Walker, Jr. and Eric Thomas Thank you, is not enough! Your friendship, mentorship, encouragement and support is greatly appreciated.

To my wife Alex, I am so blessed to have a partner like you. You are my best friend and soul mate. I love you for all that you do, have done and continue to do. I appreciate your support of everything I do. We are truly blessed and it is...

"A Beautiful Thing!"

Words of Encouragement...

The words that come out of your mouth provide the environment you create around yourself. Be sure that when you speak, positive and encouraging words are being shared. Too often we discourage ourselves and others by what we say... "You'll never make it." "Think realistically." "Stick to what you know best." But what if what you know best is not your passion?

How about saying... "You can do whatever your heart desires." "I can see you being successful at that..." Or, just simply... "I'm praying that it will all work out for you, and I support whatever it is you want to do."

There are times we need motivation, and the only way to receive words of encouragement is to give those same words to someone who needs them just as badly as you do. How would things be if we all supported one another, and kept a positive outlook on what it is we want to accomplish? The windows of opportunities and blessings would be wide open.

Please take the time as often as you can, if not everyday, to give someone a positive word of encouragement. Take the time out to let someone know they are doing well and to keep up the good work. Let someone know that you are proud of them. This type of positive reinforcement is very important and necessary. Watch it spread and you'll see love spread as well. I want you to walk away from this book with the understanding that "Love and Success Are a Lifestyle!"

Keep doing what you are doing, and making your dreams come true. The only way to predict the future is to create it. Keep your head up, and a smile on your face. This is your season, so step your game up.

What Is Success?

Success is realized when you are able to balance everything: family, friends, career, and extracurricular activities. When those around you are satisfied, when those around you are inspired, that is where true success will find you. What is business success if you have no one to share it with, and are not able to enjoy it?

Never consider yourself a success if those around you are not successful or inspired by your passion for what you do or have achieved. Think of it as; "The sum is greater than the whole of its parts." The ability to make all things work in conjunction with one another is the ultimate challenge and goal, but it is the best pay-off ever.

After having an in depth conversation with a few friends a week ago. I realized that I had more potential than I could imagine. It's funny as you go about life, and accomplish certain things you tend to forget how blessed you truly are. Never once did I think that I could not be good at something. But never did I think that I could possibly waste a few blessings along the way.

My friends and I spoke about what happens to a person when he or she gets bored. Bored with life, school, marriage, and career. It seems as we look back and think about things that were near and dear to us, we might have had opportunities that we took for granted. Have you ever been so good at something that you never thought to challenge yourself to further greatness? Have you missed the opportunity to put some spark into your relationship or marriage? Too smart to attempt to challenge yourself so you just waited for the rest of the class to catch up while you got distracted by things that did not need your attention? How much further would we be in life had we only stuck to something, and challenged ourselves to become even better?

We cannot change the past. Who we are today is because of what we did yesterday, but we can strive to be even better tomorrow. With technology much further advanced than it has been in the past you can dream bigger than ever. There are role models, and idols that are doing what some of us wish we had the confidence to do or just the discipline to apply ourselves. Make a change today! Pick up on the passion that you once had, and see where it can take you. If you believe that it is too late then encourage our young people to do so. Let them know they can do anything they so desire if they put their minds to it. However, help them to understand that it will take faith, patience, and trust to accomplish these things. It may come easy. It may be more difficult than others, but always challenge yourself to become better than you were the day before.

Yes!

Create Your Own Luck...

You create your own luck. Based on your own decisions, you create what happens to you. You create your future, both by your actions and your non-actions.

Positive Thoughts...

It is only when you begin to replace negative thoughts and behavior with positive thoughts and behavior that you will start to see positive things happen for you. It will change you, and those around you. Be a positive source of inspiration.

Know What You Want In Order To Be Successful.

Know what you want. Understand what you're doing. Love what you're doing. Believe in what you're doing... It is pretty simple, don't make it complicated.

Risk It All...

To win it all sometimes you have to risk it all. You'll never know what you can accomplish unless you try to go for it, and put it all on the line.

Inspiration!

*Are you inspired today? Have you inspired someone
close to you today? You should be inspired every
day. Just to wake up, and live to see another day is
inspiration enough for us. But be sure to inspire someone
else if only by your actions.*

Follow The Leader...

There is a difference between following followers and following leaders. The difference is extraordinary.

Chance of Success...

Your chances of success are directly connected to the degree of pleasure you derive from what you love to do.

Failing...

Failing doesn't make you a failure. Giving up and accepting that you have failed, and refusing to gather up the courage to try again does.

Have A Goal...

A goal without a plan is just a wish.
Plan, Plot, Strategize and then Execute.

Change...

If you can't change the people that are around you, change the people that are around you.

Great!

Great vs. Good

Never let great be the enemy of good.
A good decision made quickly is far better than
a great decision made slowly.

Fear vs. Belief...

You can't make it until you BELIEVE you can make it. The most successful people in the world have a NO FEAR attitude and a sense of entitlement. Others FEAR success and BELIEVE they might not have a chance at anything. Why not you? Don't be afraid. BELIEVE!

No Dress Rehearsal...

There is NO dress rehearsal for life. We live in the 'Here and Now'. In these days, tomorrow is not promised. Live life to the fullest. Love with all your heart. Keep family and good friends close. Make money & Share with those in need. Go hard, go home or watch the rest of us get Busy!

Tunnel Vision...

If you're going to move forward, you can't look behind you. Stay focused on your goal and not the static noise from around you or behind you. You can't make any progress if you don't focus on the road ahead of you.

Blessed & Gifted...

Build on your strengths that you are blessed with so that they become second nature. Some say luck is when opportunity comes along and you're prepared for it. Luck comes and goes, but when you're blessed and gifted you can do the impossible.

Right vs. Best...

When in doubt follow your gut, and do what makes you happy. But remember the right thing to do isn't always the best thing to do. And the best thing to do isn't always the right thing.

The Good and the Bad...

Never be afraid to grow when life is good or in the times of adversity. Be grateful and appreciative of the best and worst of times. You deserve the good, and learn from the bad. Never over-celebrate your blessings, and never walk out on yourself when times are bad.

Sense of Urgency!!!

Your sense of urgency isn't that of the next man or woman. Do what you have to do to become successful. Relying on others compromises your goals. Don't get upset that they can't move when you need to make moves... Their time isn't yours, and not a priority. Do what you need to do!

Don't Wonder... Just Do!

Don't sit and wonder why good things never happen to you. Don't ask why you can't catch a break. Good things happen for those who refuse to lose. Keep Pushing. Keep Praying. Be Passionate. Be Productive, and Stay Positive!

Live Well With Others...

Learn to live well with family and friends. Create a lifetime of great memories. So when we get to an age when we are no longer able to drive a nice car, live in a big house, and wear the expensive clothes, you will have these memories with the ones you love, well after the material things are gone.

Forgive!

Forgive and Forget...

Leave the past where it is. Sometimes we focus on the negative things too much. Forgive and Forget is the thing to do. Some say they may forgive, but never will they forget. Well, you can't have a better tomorrow if you're thinking about yesterday. You can't attract positive energy when you're consumed with negativity.

Struggle Hard!

Struggle as hard as you can for whatever you believe in. It is in the struggle that you will find your passion, beliefs, and your heart have to work as one to accomplish the goals you set for yourself to become successful.

Problems vs. Solutions...

The problem is not that there are problems. The problem is expecting and thinking that having problems is a problem. But there really aren't any problems, just solutions. To think otherwise is a problem... Change your perspective!

Want More Than The Best...

Some people are willing to live with the best the world can provide. For some that's not always good enough. You should push for nothing short of perfection.

Thinking the Right Way...

Thinking the right things is very critical to where we want to be and where we want to go. If you think things won't get any better 10 times out of 10 they will not. If you believe they can only get better, then you are on your way and open to the possibilities that lie ahead to make you successful.

Practice Makes Perfect...

Practice makes perfect! If you practice mediocrity you will achieve mediocre qualities. Practice greatness you achieve great distinction. Life isn't a dress rehearsal; there is no pre-season and no 'do-over'. Practice hard, play hard.

Just Be the Best You...

You don't have to be the greatest Doctor, Lawyer, Dentist, Entertainer, Athlete, Mother or Father. Just be the BEST you that you can be, it's a great feeling!

Live!

Live / Love / Life...

*Live what you love and you will
find life is worth living.*

Be Contagious!

The funny thing about success is that it can be contagious. Inspire those around you with the way you smile and carry yourself as a successful individual. As you do that those around you want to know what it is, and how to get that feeling of success. It starts with inspiring others with your journey, and your testimony.

Live A Good Life...

When you reach the later years of your life, it is the relationships and memories you have developed, and created that make you truly happy and fulfilled. So it is wise to live well with others so that when you look back you can be proud to know you have no regrets.

What Matters Most...

Don't be one of those people who neglect family and health while pursuing success. Being successful and having money is important, but it really isn't worth losing the things that really matter the most at the end of the day.

Who Pays The Bill...?

True success is when you and those around you are successful. It's when you go out to eat and fight about who's gonna pay the bill. Not, who's gonna pay the bill...?

Failure vs. Success...

The difference between success and failure is forgetting about yesterday, and starting today. Not procrastinating today, waiting for the opportune time to make it happen tomorrow.

Gotta Have Faith...

You can lose your job, house, car, and friends. But whatever happens—as long as you live to see another day, and have your health and strength—never lose your faith.

Success Is A Choice!

Today is the perfect day for CHANGE. Today is your day to take one step towards your goals and dreams. Imagine it, living life on your terms, doing what you want, when you want, and loving every minute of it. It is possible. You can have everything you want in life, but you have to take control, and make it work for you. Success is a choice!

Have Vision...

It's not how good you are right now. It's how good you want to be that matters. Take the time to Plan, Plot & Strategize a vision of where you want to be and make it a reality. Nothing is impossible!

Have A Forgiving Heart...

The biggest obstacle most people face is forgiveness! Forgiveness of self and others. Don't allow pride and ego to get in the way of forgiving yourself and others close to you. A misunderstanding or an unfortunate situation will block your blessings.

Value Important Relationships...

It is important to value relationships with friends and loved ones as you journey toward success. These relationships will be the ones which sustain you well after all that you accomplish along the way.

The Importance of Time...

Time: There are so many perspectives. Time waits for no man or woman. Time is of the essence. The Time is now! When the Time is right! All of these and many are true. But one thing for sure; nothing can happen before its Time. So success is based on if you're ready when the Time comes.

Insecurity Is A Hindrance...

It is our own insecurities, and not the insecurity of others that hold us back from our potential to succeed in Life, Love or Business.

Let Go of The Past...

When you let go of past experiences—bad or good, you open up yourself to a world of new experiences that can change your perspective and direction in life. Let go, and explore what is available to you. The possibilities are endless.

Get Out Of The Way!

Do yourself a favor and stay out of the way of your blessings. Instead of thinking, "Why Me?" Start saying "Why Not Me!"

Realize!

Realize Those Who Add Value...

There are people we can live with and those we can live without. The key is to realize the value in those we cannot live without, and admit that those we can live without don't add value to our journey in life or our success.

Determination...

One of the most important things in life is having the determination to succeed. With that determination, you force yourself to adjust and accept situations that would make the average person quit. Be determined and inspire those around you to be better than the average.

Passion into Action...

Make today the last day you allow life and its mundane perspective to stifle the things you love, and are passionate about. Find time to turn your passions into action. You'll discover more success on things that you are passionate about, more so than things you have to do just to get a paycheck.

Material Investment...

Don't look for material things to justify your position or status in life, and amongst your family & friends. Invest in materials things that help to create long lasting memories.

No Need to Give Up...

There's no need to give up on your dreams, and aspirations for something that's probably not going to be good for you anyway. Stay on your path. Endure the storms, and the setbacks. The experience is part of the journey. The satisfaction of success, and the payoff will be more than worth it.

Get Your Mind Right!

Success in life is based more on your mental attitude than on your mental capabilities. Only you can create your own disposition. Until that happens, you allow others to create your realities. People who manage their attitude avoid being managed by others. Get your mind right, and the rest will fall in place.

It's Never Too Late...

Think about your life, and what you want to accomplish. Choose something you are passionate about. After careful thought, and consideration take personal responsibility for your decision. Then create your own success. It's never too late to start.
You just have to start today.

Think It, Believe It, Speak It...

The words that come out of your mouth provide the environment you create around yourself. If you want to be successful in life, relationships and business you have to speak those things into existence. To achieve it, you must believe it. To believe it then you first must speak it.

Present Blessing...

Don't look past the present blessings you have in front of you. The more we strive for greatness and success—the more we will experience more blessings. But to enjoy them one day at a time while we can is what is most important.

The Taste of Success...

A taste of success is different from having an appetite for it. Once you realize all that goes into becoming successful at something, you'll appreciate why it is an acquired taste for only a chosen few. Some people find it difficult to be successful and happy at the same time. Are you hungry for success and happiness?

Appreciate!

Appreciate Everything Around You...

It takes a lifetime to appreciate everyone, and everything along this journey we experience called life. In these days and times a lifetime is a long time. And most of us never get enough time to appreciate anything. Take the time today, and appreciate all that you can in life.

What Are You Leaving Behind...

When it is all said and done what will people remember the most about you? Plant the seeds today that will continue to grow far beyond your existence. Leave a legacy of greatness that inspires people to achieve a level of success that continues to be infectious. Be the best you, and always do the best that you can.

The Possible and Impossible...

The difference between those that succeed and those that barely make it, is the effort to do both the possible and impossible. The impossible is just as easy as the possible if you don't over-think it or talk yourself out of it.

Where Do You Stand Today?

You are not the only one who has experienced where you stand now. Where you stand now, and where you stand tomorrow should never be the same. Ask the person in front of you or behind you, where they have been, and where they are going. The answer for your next move lies between those answers. Just listen.

Don't Wait To Celebrate Life!

Good things come to those who wait. But blessings come to those who never wait to share their successes and failures with the people who matter the most. Those people are the friends and family you keep close. The ones that love you regardless of your accomplishments. Choose these people wisely, and treat them properly as well. You should celebrate life with them, every chance you get!

Live Outside The Box!

If you want to live outside the box be sure to have a circle of friends who support, and love you. You will find that sometimes the ones that say they love you are the same ones who try to keep you boxed in. Sometimes you don't realize it is your loved ones who are guilty of this same behavior. Know your worth, but most importantly see to it that others know it as well. Refuse to live in a box!

You Don't Have To Answer Verbally...

There should never be a question as to whether you will be successful or not. The only question should be how successful will you be. Period! No need to verbally answer the question, just let your actions speak louder than your words. However, if you feel the need to say anything just simply reply, "I am walking in my blessings on the way to my goals and success, and I hope to see you there!"

When One Door Closes...

They say when one door closes another is open. The question is are you gonna knock on the door or do you just walk in boldly? Those who are truly successful walk in like they kicked the door down.

Winning Combination...

Competence, experience, and a positive mental attitude make up a winning combination. Make sure you have the right components needed to succeed. Without them your chances become somewhat slim, and you risk the inevitable—failure.

Try!

Try And Fail...

Some people try and fail. Some fail to try. Some can't help but fail. Some try, and try again, and then they quit. The successful people are the ones who never stop trying, and are not afraid to fail in order to one day succeed.

Calling Audibles...

If you are trying to figure out or predict your future, it can be easier than you think. Write down your dreams, goals, and aspirations. That is your blueprint to success or lack there of. Plan your work—work your plan. You can predict the outcome if you follow your game plan, but you'll have to call a few 'audibles' along the way to success.

Audible: *A play called at the line of scrimmage to supersede the play originally agreed upon as the result of a change in strategy.*

Keep Right-Minded People Around...

Sometimes the biggest challenge is to not lose focus of your goals. Keep positive, like-minded people in your circle. You can't afford to have negative people around, they are a waste of time, and money.

Dreaming While Awake...

You don't have to fall asleep to dream. Close your eyes every now and again, and dream the wildest and most amazing things. If you believe in them they come true. When they do come true, life will feel like a dream. But don't sleep, your dreams only come true if you work on them.

Success Is A Lifestyle!

The key to success in life is living it as a lifestyle. It means doing the small things now that feel right, and not just those that look right. Successful people remain successful and attract success because they live it as a lifestyle, and not because it's in style.

Barriers Limit Blessings...

Many of us have barriers which limit our thinking and as a result make our personal and professional growth stagnant. Don't be the individual in the room that has remained the same over the years because of the barriers you put up around yourself. You're too busy putting people in a box, and not realizing you are boxing yourself in. Let the sun shine in. Don't block your blessings!

Money Vs. Time

The greatest asset in life isn't money. It is time.
Be sure to cherish it before it runs out.

Fear of Change...

Change is good! Oftentimes it is God presenting or offering a different perspective. Embrace it, and move forward. Most people fear the unknown. Don't be afraid! The only thing that remains constant in this universe is change.

Why Wait?

It is said, "Good things come to those who wait." Great things happen for those who have an action plan. Don't wait for something good to happen when you can create great things right now!

Dream!

Dream Your Game plans...

Take time to figure out a game plan for your dreams. The longer you take to figure that out, the longer the dream remains just that. A dream can only end when reality takes over. Most of us walk around dreaming and put nothing to action because the lack of a plan. Plan today to make your dreams come true tomorrow.

New Perspective...

Find interest in things unfamiliar to you, to gain a new perspective and understanding. You only know what you know. But you can learn about what you don't know, and that makes the difference in those who choose to be succesful, and those who end up stagnant.

Packaged Blessings...

Don't block your blessings! There are others who would die to have the blessings you take for granted! One person's burden is a blessing to someone else. Blessings come in different forms not always in a pretty package with a bow, but a blessing none-the-less.

Learning How To Count...

We count on the wrong things at times. We count our money. We count on friends and family. Nothing is wrong with that, but the truth is we should concentrate on what matters most, and on things that really count. Count your blessings before they run out.

Think Optimistically...

Instead of being disappointed about where you are in life, right now. Think optimistically about where you are going or want to go. You will run into roadblocks at various points, and stops in life. However, always keep in mind that adversity is not a dead-end or a reason to stop, but more like a detour to a better outcome along your journey.

Live Your Best Life!

Each day you wake up to live and see another day there is one important thing to remember. You only have one ride through life so you might as well enjoy it. Keep in mind, life is a gift and not an obligation. Live your best life!

Motivating Others...

Find a way to motivate and inspire your family and friends to achieve success in anything that they are passionate about. The results will amaze you. What you come to find out is that you are motivated, and at the same time realize your own passion. Every once in a good while we all need motivation, and 'a swift kick in the pants'.

Maybe You Should Or Maybe Not...

Maybe you should, maybe you should'nt. Think it over, but never let it end up becoming a 'maybe I should have' or 'maybe I should not have' situation. Consider the outcome whether it is good or bad before putting action to your thoughts. Most times you have one chance to make it happen, and no time to undo or redo it.

Character Is...

Character is believing in yourself when others don't. It is having the ability to not allow that to disrupt your master plan, and the big picture to succeed.

Share!

Share Your Vision, Magic Happens...

Find people that make things happen rather then trust those that make excuses about why things can't happen. Share your vision only with those who understand your dreams. That is when the magic will happen and those around you will help make those dreams turn into realities.

You Know What's Best...

It is not what people around you are telling you that matters most. Those are just opinions from different perspectives to be considered or not. But it is the voice from within you that should be paid close attention to. Not everyone knows what is best for you as well as you do.

Anytime Spring Cleaning...

We worry too much about those that hate on our dreams and goals, but forget about those that hinder our growth. You can keep the haters at a distance, but the hinderers are among us. They may be a spouse, boyfriend, girlfriend, best friend or relative. No hard feelings, it's never too late for spring-cleaning!

Quality Of Life Perspective...

You can make a difference in the quality of life for yourself and others important to you by just having the proper perspective and outlook of life. Always remember, it is not what you have that matters but what you can share with others that is important. When you get rid of all the stuff, make sure what you have left is substance, memories and meaningful friendships.
That is a good life!

No Do-Overs...

Most of the time there is no next time, no second chance, no do-over, no dress rehearsal. Most times it is simply do or die, now or never. Be prepared when opportunities come knocking, and windows/doors open.

Your Heart's Passion...

When you find what your heart is most passionate about, you find happiness. True happiness, and success are found right around the corner from passion, and next door to inspiration. If you make it there mentally you will find yourself in the right neighborhood.

Pay Attention To The Right People...

You would be surprised to know there are more people that want to see you succeed than those that want you to fail. The thing most of us don't realize is that we are at fault for paying attention to the nay-sayers, instead of the ones that want to see us win. Let's start to focus on the right things, and the right people in our lives.

Stay In Your Lane...

Never mind the business of others and what they are doing to use as some kind of measurement or report card of where you need to be or what you need to be doing. Stay in your own lane and that is where you will find continued success. Remember it is not a race to see who finishes first, but it is to see who lasts the longest.

The Perfect Bigger Picture...

In order to be happy you have to understand the bigger picture. To be truly successful at anything you must see the big picture. To enjoy life to the fullest you have to realize everyday isn't gonna be picture perfect. Some people get the picture while others find themselves, well... Out of the picture.

Accomplish What Is Important But...

It is important to have goals to accomplish, and the ability to achieve them. The proper perspective is to achieve the ones that matter most and count towards your being happy and satisfied. You don't have to complete everything you dream or plan, only to jeopardize being happy in the process or losing friends and loved ones along the way. Create memories that will last a lifetime.

What If ?

You never have to worry about the "What If's" in life when you live life to the fullest. When it is all said and done, the only regret you should have is not doing what you love, and loving those you care about most, ten times more than you already did. Live your best life as best you can. Always!

Keep Quiet When Necessary...

Know when to keep quiet. But more importantly, know when to speak up. You don't have to speak to always get your point across. However, choose your words and timing correctly to make a monumental statement when you do speak. The tongue is a double-edged sword. Use it when necessary. Use it wisely.
Use it to inspire!

Nobody Is Perfect Without Trying...

Nobody's perfect. But everybody's trying. Try is the operative word. Nothing beats a failure, but a try. Don't make a power point presentation out of other peoples lives when yours wouldn't look so good on the evening news. Nobody's perfect. But everybody's trying. Encourage and inspire them to keep trying.

Who's Better?

Who's better than you? Be the best you can be at all times, and you never have to compete with anyone but yourself.

No More Excuses...

Don't allow anyone to give you any excuses. It's only a matter of time before they lie to you, if they haven't already. Set the standard to what you will, and will not tolerate. More importantly, don't make excuses or lie to yourself.

Create Your Own Path...

When you follow the path of others, you have to understand that is their journey. It is only when you get lost and have to find your own way that you realize your journey is much different than that of others. Don't be afraid to get lost, make mistakes, and learn your own lessons. There is no other way to achieve the success that belongs to you.

Right Place, Right Time.

There is a time, and a place for everything. When that time comes you must be cognizant of what to say, and what to do. It is more than just using common sense. It is using your heart, mind, and soul that allows you to make the right decisions. All while keeping in mind that the right thing to do, isn't always the best thing to do. And the best thing to do, isn't always the right thing to do.

Your Undivided Attention Is Needed...

When in doubt, go with your gut feeling. If your sixth sense is telling you something, more than likely whatever the situation is, it will require more detailed attention. Interpretation: Always pay attention, and try to feel things out. Better yet, give certain situations your undivided attention.

Get What You Deserve...

There are times you will have to be selfish, and take what you deserve. If you wait around for others to give it to you then you might be waiting a long time. Even worse, you might be disappointed with the results, and the efforts of those individuals. Everyone doesn't believe in give and take. Some just take.

Make No Comparison...

Don't compare your life to others around you. You have no idea what their journey is all about. The only thing you have in common with others is your opportunity to make the best of every day given to you. The only comparison that would really matter would be who made it happen Vs. who didn't.

Finding Inspiration

They say you find inspiration in the strangest and most interesting places. All you have to do is open up your heart, mind, and soul. When the light shines within, the light shines even brighter when it comes out.

Simply, Don't Forget...

Never allow yourself to become overwhelmed or consumed by your day to day responsibilities that you forget to simply appreciate, and enjoy life. You have one life to live. Live it one day at a time.
One moment at a time.

Make It A Day To Remember...

Make it a day to remember! If not, make it a day the devil, the haters, and the nay-sayers will never forget!

Think BIG Picture...

If you know where you want to be one day, you have to be honest with yourself as to where you are, today. It matters not how long it takes you to get there or what direction you take. All that matters is that you keep the destination in sight at all times. Some will tell you that you are going in the wrong direction, that it is taking too long, that there is no light at the end of the journey. How would they know? It's not their journey. It is your destiny alone to direct with the help of like-minded people that believe in the big picture you have in mind.

Don't Be Surprised...

It might be a surprise how hard it is for most people to be happy for the success of others. Blessings come abundantly to those you support others good fortune without feeling like they wish it were them. Feel blessed with what you have not envious of what you don't. There are people who wish to have just half of what you have.

Finish!

Finish What You Start!

Once you begin your journey make sure you go all the way. Half-hearted efforts will not be enough. Either you give your all or leave well enough alone. There are those who are looking from the sidelines waiting for you to either succeed or fail. Make sure your efforts are not in vain, and deliver more than people expect!

Take Time To Think...

Find a quiet place where you can sit and think. Then ask yourself some questions about who you are, and where you are going in your life. There is nothing you cannot do, and nothing you cannot have. Making sure you know what you want, and how to get it is essential to ensure ultimate success, when you dedicate time to think it through.

Giving Up Is Easy!

On this journey we call life there will be times when you feel like giving up. The moment you feel like giving up can be the moment you recieve your breakthrough. It seems like most people these days are willing to give up too easy. You ever wonder how most successful people made it to where they are today? Determination, Stubborness, Tenacity, Mental toughness, and most importantly the stamina to not give up too easy or too soon. Imagine waking up to find out the day you gave up, your blessing was sitting right at your front door, but you never went to answer. Now the blessing says: Return To Sender.

Speak Life Into What You Want!

If you want to achieve great things, speak them into existence. If you don't, the same rules apply. Ten times out of ten if you think the reverse of the first action, failure is sure to follow.

Impossibility Does Not Exist...

Impossible does not exist to those that believe in their abilities. For them, the possibilities are endless because their belief in those abilities makes anything and everything possible. Keep in mind the word itself... The Possible + Your Abilities = Possibilities!

Inspire!

Inspire Someone!

Inspire someone today! Do it because it feels good. Do it because someone needs it. Do it no matter who is watching. You'll begin to realize how being an inspiration to others allows you to become inspired and fuels that thing which you are most passionate about.

The key word: Inspire

*Being positive doesn't require a lot.
All it takes is an open Heart, positive Mind
and a pure Soul.*

And if you were still wondering...
Yes, *Every Day Can Be A Good Day!*

The End

Keys...
To Success

Stop holding onto things you need to let go of. Most of the things we tend to hold onto the most are the very same things that are holding us back. The moment you release those things or persons is when you receive your blessings and favour beyond belief. Start letting go today! You can't continue to carry everything and everyone on your journey that doesn't add value or purpose.

Keys...
To Success

Sometimes bad things are the best things that can happen to us. How we adapt and embrace them will determine our success. Once you realize your steps are ordered that is when your window of blessings and opportunities will be wide open. The key to attract more is to make sure others who deserve it, have access to those same things as well. Blessings in life or business should be shared, and not coveted.

Today is the day to hug someone tight. Tell someone you love them with all your heart. Do something for someone that will make them smile. Call someone far away that you love, and tell them you were thinking of them. Tell someone you appreciate and honor them. Pray for someone. Do something that brings you closer to your dreams, happiness, and being successful. Take a deep breath, and be thankful to see another day! Do all of these things today, like it was your last day on earth. Because one day it will come, and it would have been too late to do any of these things.
Don't wait!

Keys...
To Success

It is never too late to be who it is that you want to be.
Your dreams don't have an expiration date. However,
the longer you wait, the harder it is to make those
dreams a reality. Start today because tomorrow
isn't promised to all of us.

Keys...
To Success

Find or create your piece of the pie that feeds your appetite to succeed. Take a bite out of it everyday to get you going the minute you wake up!

Keys...
To Success

Technology will get you through the day, but it can't help you navigate through your life. Success is best found following the blueprint designed by how you feel in your gut, and in your spirit. When looking for happiness and success there is no 5-Star review to read. Google Maps and GPS can't help you. Follow your heart. It will always put you on the right path.

Never allow yourself to become overwhelmed or consumed by your day to day responsibilities that you forget to simply appreciate, and enjoy life. You have one life to live. Live it one day at a time. One moment at a time.

Keys...
To Success

In order to succeed at anything your approach must contain Faith, Patience, and Trust. These key pieces must be woven into the fabric of your being, and added as a protection of armor to fend off the individuals and things that cross the path along your journey. Do Not allow anyone or anything to shake your Faith, allow you to become impatient or lose trust in yourself, your abilities, and your dreams. You are the writer, producer, and director of your Life.
Make it a blockbuster smash!

CPSIA information can be obtained
at www.ICGtesting.com
Printed in the USA
LVOW04n0844190117
521513LV00005B/16/P